Don't Forget!

May Day

Monica Hughes

Heinemann
LIBRARY

www.heinemann.co.uk/library
Visit our website to find out more information about **Heinemann Library** books.

To order:
 Phone 44 (0) 1865 888066
 Send a fax to 44 (0) 1865 314091
 Visit the Heinemann Bookshop at www.heinemann.co.uk/library to browse our
catalogue and order online.

First published in Great Britain by Heinemann Library, Halley Court, Jordan Hill, Oxford
OX2 8EJ, a division of Reed Educational and Professional Publishing Ltd. Heinemann is a
registered trademark of Reed Educational and Professional Publishing Ltd.

OXFORD MELBOURNE AUCKLAND JOHANNESBURG BLANTYRE
GABORONE IBADAN PORTSMOUTH NH (USA) CHICAGO

© Reed Educational and Professional Publishing Ltd 2002
First published in paperback in 2003
The moral right of the proprietor has been asserted.

Designed by Joanna Sapwell and StoryBooks
Originated by Ambassador Litho Ltd
Printed in China by Wing King Tong

ISBN 0 431 15400 7 (hardback)   ISBN 0 431 15407 4 (paperback)
06 05 04 03 02   07 06 05 04 03
10 9 8 7 6 5 4 3 2 1   10 9 8 7 6 5 4 3 2 1

British Library Cataloguing in Publication Data
Hughes, Monica
        May Day. – (Don't Forget)
        1. May Day – Juvenile literature
        I.Title
        394 . 2'64

Acknowledgements
The Publishers would like to thank the following for permission to reproduce photographs: Bridgeman Art
Library/Christies Images p. 17; Bridgeman Art Library/Thyssen-Bornemisza Collection, Madrid, Spain p. 24;
Collections/Brian Shuel pp. 14, 18, 20, 22; Collections/Gordon Hill pp. 5, 9, 12, 15; Collections/Robert Pilgrim
p. 19; Collections/Vi p. 16; Corbis p.7; Corbis/Adam Woolfitt p. 10; Getty Images/FPG p. 23; Getty Images/Stone
pp. 8, 11; Hulton Getty p. 13; Katz p. 27; Lebrecht Music Collection p. 26; Photodisc p. 29; Robert Harding p. 4;
Southern Daily Echo p. 21; Topham Picturepoint/Imageworks p. 28; Trevor Clifford p. 25; Tropix p. 6.

Cover photograph reproduced with permission of Pictures of Britain.

Our thanks to Stuart Copeman for his assistance in the preparation of this book.

Permission was kindly granted by Macmillan for the extract from *The Green Man in the Garden*
by Charles Causley.

Every effort has been made to contact copyright holders of any material reproduced in this book. Any
omissions will be rectified in subsequent printings if notice is given to the Publishers.

Contents

Words printed in bold letters, **like this**, are explained in the Glossary.

What is May Day?

The first day of the month of May is known as May Day. It is the time of year when warmer weather begins and flowers and trees start to blossom. It is said to be a time of love and **romance**. It is when people celebrate the coming of summer with lots of different **customs** that are expressions of joy and hope after a long winter.

In some places May Day celebrations begin at sunset on 30 April. They include lots of **floral** decorations and processions through towns and villages. There are often different kinds of music, dancing and dressing up. May Day is great fun for all involved.

Children carrying garlands of flowers on May Day

Maypole dancing is very popular on May Day

The first day of May is not the only special day in the month. Throughout May different days, especially Saturdays, are set aside for May Day celebrations in places across Britain. The first Monday nearest the May Day is a **bank holiday** and the time for many people to enjoy a spring break from school or work.

When is May Day?

May Day is now the first day of the month of May. But before 1752, when the calendar was changed, it was 11 days earlier.

5

What were May Days like in the past?

Celebrations have been held at the beginning of May for thousands of years. The Romans held a six-day festival at the end of April and the beginning of May called *Floralia*. They gathered flowers as offerings to Flora, the **goddess** of springtime.

The **Celtic** fire festival of 'Beltane' was celebrated at this time of year. On the eve of May Day, bonfires were lit on hilltops throughout Britain. In many homes all the other fires were put out. Flaming branches from the bonfire were used to relight the fires on May Day morning.

Bonfires were once common on May Day

May Day was the day when farmers moved their animals to their summer **pastures**. The animals were driven in a procession with the sheep leading, then the cattle, followed by the goats and finally the horses. This was usually accompanied by singing, dancing and feasting.

Maia is one of the Seven Sisters star cluster

May goddesses

The month of May is named after the Roman **Earth Mother**, Maia. She was thought to be the mother of **fertile** soil and responsible for new growth in spring. The Greeks also had a goddess called Maia. She is thought to be one of the stars that appear in the middle of May.

What are maypoles?

There are records of maypoles in England from around the 1400s. Young men and women, known as 'mayers' used to go into the woods before May Day. They would search for a tall straight tree like a birch or an ash. They would bring the tree back, leaving some greenery at the top, and put it up for people to dance around.

Maypole dancing at Leeds Castle, Kent

Famous maypoles

The maypole in Ansty, Wiltshire is 15 metres (50 feet) tall. The previous maypole was 30 metres (98 feet) tall and thought to be the tallest in England. The maypole in Barwick-in-Elmet in Yorkshire stays in place all year. It is taken down and repainted every three years.

Maypole dancing is still a popular part of many celebrations on May Day. Different coloured ribbons hang from the top of the pole. The dancers each hold a ribbon and weave in and out of each other, around the Maypole. As they dance the ribbons make a colourful plait down the pole. The dance ends with the dancers going in the opposite direction, and unplaiting the ribbons.

The top of a maypole decorated with flowers

9

 # What is morris dancing?

Traditional Derby morris dancing

There are often displays of morris dancing in town squares and on village greens at this time of year. The dancing is very lively and often accompanied by an **accordion** player.

Morris dancers are usually men and wear different clothes depending on the area in which they dance. They are often dressed in white with coloured **baldrics** across their chests. Sometimes their clothes are covered in coloured strips of cloth called 'tatters'.

Dancing a jig

Morris dancing is probably named after a Spanish **jig** called the *Morisco*. There are many different morris dances but they usually include lots of noise, stamping of feet and leaping in the air. The dancers were believed to scare away evil **spirits** and guarantee a good summer.

A morris dancer with bells on his legs and wearing a hat decorated with flowers

There are usually six or eight dancers arranged in two lines or in a circle facing each other. The dancers may carry white handkerchiefs that they shake, or short sticks that they bang against each other as they dance.

There are also single dancers who wear special clothes. One of the dancers might be a **hobby horse**, and wear a tall animal mask and a cloak covering their head and shoulders. There may also be a 'fool', dressed as a woman, who dances in and out of the sides and is often the leader of the dancers.

11

 # Who is the May queen?

A May queen surrounded by flowers

A May queen is an important person in many May Day celebrations. She is a local girl chosen for one year by other children. She dresses in white and carries a bouquet of fresh flowers. Younger children act as her attendants, and are called maids in waiting.

The May queen leads the May Day procession. Sometimes she may ride in a horse-drawn carriage or on a decorated **float**. When she arrives at the field or park where the celebrations take place, she sits on a flower-covered throne. A crown-bearer, usually a young boy, offers the crown from the previous year to the new queen .

The 1937 May queen of all England, Dorothy Smead

The new May queen is crowned and there is much applause. The new queen then watches the maypole dancing and other attractions. In a large May fair these often include bands, a fun fair, food and sweet stalls and sideshows.

The May Queen by Tennyson

You must wake and call me early, call me early, mother dear;
Tomorrow'll be the happiest time of all the glad New-year, –
Of all the glad New-year, mother, the maddest, merriest day;
For I'm to be Queen o' the May, mother, I'm to be queen o' the May.

Have you ever seen a hobby horse?

The **hobby horse** is a special May Day animal. It is not a real animal, but a model or a costume and it is used by morris dancers and in May Day processions. Sometimes it doesn't even look like a horse at all!

An unusual hobby horse can be seen in Padstow, Cornwall. It is called Old 'Oss. It is almost 2 metres (6 feet) wide, black, with a circular hoop covered in canvas and a skirt hanging all round it. It has a horse's head at the front with snapping jaws and a small tail at the back.

The Padstow hobby horse

Blue Ribbon is the name of another Padstow hobby horse. It is a bit bigger than Old 'Oss but the same shape. It has a white beard and red, white and blue ribbons fixed around the hoop.

The Minehead Sailor's Horse

Both horses swoop and swirl madly about as a 'teaser' leads them around the town collecting money for charity. The teaser is a man carrying a club or stick.

Another hobby horse

In Minehead, North Devon there is a hobby horse called the Sailor's Horse. It is boat shaped and multi-coloured. The top is covered with strips of cloth, which flutter when the horse shakes himself. It has a tall hat decorated with ribbons and feathers, and a long tail that trails on the ground.

Why did people 'bring in the may'?

The evening before May Day was thought to be lucky. On this night, or early on May Day morning, young people went into the woods to look for flowering branches to bring home at sunrise. This was known as 'bringing in the may'. The people were called 'mayers' and were said to be going 'a maying'.

'May' was any tree in blossom by May Day. In many places this was the hawthorn, but in Cornwall it was the sycamore. In Scotland, Wales and northern England the may was the rowan or mountain ash.

Hawthorn blossom, also called May blossom

16

May Day, an oil painting by James Hayllar (1829–1920)

The flowering branches were often carried from house to house, accompanied by singing. The may was then used to decorate the houses to celebrate the coming of summer. The mayers hoped they would then be offered food, drink or money.

Flowers were also gathered and used in the decorations, or to make **garlands** or **posies**.

Garland Day

Garland Day is held in Abbotsbury in Dorset. Children carry garlands on poles round the village visiting different houses. The garlands are about 60 centimetres (2 feet) tall and bell shaped, with a pole pushed through the middle. One garland is decorated with wild flowers and another with garden flowers.

Who is the green man?

'Jack-in-the-green' taking part in a May Day procession

A dancing man, dressed in fancy dress, leads some processions on May Day. He is known as 'Jack-in-the-green' or the green man. His costume is a wire-netting or wicker basket shaped like a **pyramid**. It is covered with leaves and decorated with branches, ribbons and flowers.

There are other names for the green man. He may be based on the ancient **Celtic** god of the hunt called Cern or Cernunnos. He is also known as the green god of nature, or the wicker man. Sometimes he is called king of the wood. He is a **symbol** of new growth in summer.

A carving of the green man from a church in Somerset

The idea of a green man who is a god of nature is very old. There are many old stone and wooden carvings of a green man on buildings, walls and churches across the country. He is shown with a beard of **vines** and flowers and with berries coming out of his mouth.

From the poem *The Green Man in the Garden* by Charles Causley

Your eyes are dark as holly,
Of sycamore your horns,
Your bones are made of elder-branch
Your teeth are made of thorns.

Your hat is made of ivy-leaf,
Of bark your dancing shoes
And evergreen and green and green,
Your jacket and shirt and trews.

19

What music is played on May Day?

Music plays an important part in the celebrations. Before dawn on May morning **choristers** climb to the top of the 44 metre (144 feet) tower of Magdalen College in Oxford and sing a hymn in **Latin**. After the singing, which includes songs called **madrigals**, the college bells ring out. The bells can be heard by the crowds who have gathered on Magdalen Bridge to celebrate 1 May.

Magdalen College, Oxford on May Day morning

Singing on the Bargate on May Day

The May Day celebrations at Magdalen College have been taking place for hundreds of years. Some think it began as a way of giving thanks for the tower, which was completed in 1509.

Singing special May Day songs has spread to a number of other places including Southampton. Here choristers from King Edward VI School sing May Day carols, at dawn, from the top of the ancient Bargate that was the gate into the medieval town.

17th-century references to May morning at Oxford

'The choral ministers of this house do according to ancient custom salute Flora every year on the first of May at four in the morning with vocal music in several parts: which, having well performed, hath given great content to the neighbourhood ...'

# Some unusual customs

'Sanding' from Knutsford, Cheshire

In Knutsford, Cheshire, there is a May Day **custom** called 'sanding'. The grounds of important buildings in the town are decorated with **mottoes** and patterns using coloured sand that has been dyed. The house of the May queen is given a special 'sanding'. Some shops and private houses are also 'sanded'. The sand eventually blows away. If it has rained on May Day (which is not unusual!) the dye from the sand soaks into the pavements and lasts for months.

Washing in May Morning **dew** is an old custom. At one time girls thought that they could improve their looks by washing their faces in dewdrops. The dew that formed on May morning was thought to be magical, and so they had to get up before dawn to collect it. The dew from hawthorn, ivy or from beneath oak trees was thought to be especially good.

Early morning mist on May Day morning

Some May Day sayings:

'Ne'er cast a clout till May be out'
    a warning against taking off warm clothes (clouts) before the end of May.
'So many mists in March, so many frosts in May'
    a warning that mists or fogs in March predicted frost in May.
'May chickens come cheeping'
    a warning that chickens born in May were weak, with feeble cries.

23

May Day food and drink

Maids of Honour cakes are associated with May Day. They are small, round puff pastry cheesecakes sometimes flavoured with almonds and **rose water**. They are thought to be a reminder of maids dancing round a maypole. Another story says that King Henry VIII found the recipe and gave it to Anne Boleyn who was a Maid of Honour. She is said to have made the cakes herself. The king named them Maids of Honour after her.

Henry VIII painted by Holbein (1497/8–1543)

Maids of Honour cakes

In the past special cakes were made on May Day and given to visitors. They were made of meat, apple, lemon, and sugar all wrapped in a pastry case. May wine was also offered to visitors. Fresh or dried meadowsweet (a meadow plant) was added to white wine and left for twenty-four hours. A May cup was a drink made by soaking dried woodruff (a sweet smelling plant) in apple juice, for fifteen minutes.

May loaves for the poor

In Geddington, Northamptonshire there was a special May bread charity set up for local poor people. On May Day they were given a special white loaf made from wheat flour to eat instead of the tougher rye or barley bread they usually ate.

May Day and Labour Day

May Day is not only used to celebrate the beginning of summer. Since 1889 it has also been used to celebrate the rights of workers. In many countries 1 May has been known as International **Labour** Day, and it is still a national holiday.

Labour Day was especially important when people worked very long hours in factories. It was a time when people could show their support for better working conditions. Every year in Britain a May Day committee organizes activities for people in **trade unions** and other workers' groups. There are speeches, parades with banners, marching bands and singing.

A marching brass band on Labour Day

More recently May Day has been used as an opportunity to **campaign** for poor people across the world. It is also a time to support looking after the **environment**.

May Day demonstration in Oxford Circus, London

Other special Labour Days

23 May – Labour Day, Jamaica
3 September – Labour Day, USA & Canada
1 October – Labour Day, New South Wales, Australia

May Day around the world

In many European countries May Day is seen as the beginning of the time for **courting**. In Italy the maypoles are known as 'trees from the land of milk and honey'. The poles are greased with lard, and then money, special ham and cheese are hung from the top. Young men try to climb the pole to get the prizes, but they can only do this after several attempts when the lard has been worn off.

German boys secretly plant May trees in front of the windows of their sweethearts, and in Switzerland a May pine is placed under a girl's window. Maypole dancing is also popular in many European countries.

Maypole dancers wearing traditional national costume in France

Many children in the USA gather flowers and put them in May baskets, which they have made out of paper. They hang the baskets on doorknobs of friends and neighbours on May morning. There are also May Day parties in parks and schools with dancing round a maypole, a May queen and May Day songs.

May Day celebrations in China are very colourful with big parades and marches. Fireworks are a noisy and attractive part of the May Day celebrations.

Fireworks are used on May Day in China

Mayday! Mayday! Mayday!

This is an international radio distress signal used by ships and aircraft. It has been in use since the 1920s. It is how you say the French word *m'aider*, which means come and help me.

Glossary

accordion portable musical instrument like a concertina

baldrics belts crossing the chest, hanging from shoulder to hip

bank holiday national holiday

campaign organized action to achieve something

Celtic belonging to the Celts, the people of ancient Britain before the Romans

choristers members of a choir

courting trying to get the love of someone

customs usual ways of doing things

dew drops of water found outside in the early morning

Earth Mother idea of a woman who was the mother of everything in nature

environment surroundings, including water, air, soil, rocks, plants and animals

fertile able to grow lots of fruit and vegetables

float lorry decorated to take part in a parade

floral having to do with flowers

garlands decorative ring of flowers

goddess female god

hobby horse stick with a horses head

jig lively dance

labour hard work

Latin language of ancient Rome

madrigals songs for several voices

Maids of Honour young woman who served a queen

mottoes short sayings or rules

pastures land covered with grass where animals graze

posies small bunches of flowers

pyramid shape with a square base and sloping
   triangular sides

romance tender feelings

rose water water perfumed by rose petals

spirits ghosts or supernatural beings

symbol sign with a special meaning

trade unions groups that help workers who work in
   the same jobs

vine climbing plant with grapes as fruit

Index